<u>Snapshot</u>

I was 5 years old, so my experience with living in, and interacting with the world, was very limited. But, in some ways that made me much more open minded. If I experienced something that was strange to me, I simply reasoned it was part of the natural order of things, and I didn't know enough to judge it and whether it fit with the way things were supposed to be. Those kinds of things usually went in the mental file labelled "forget it about for now, think about it later". I had a lot of things in that file.

The notable experience I had at age five started in May or June of 1962, the year of the Cuban Missile Crisis. One day I was sitting in the living room, watching the activity of everyday life outside our house, when a man in a military uniform of some kind appeared at the door. I say "appeared" because I did not see him walk up the drive, or the steps to the front porch; nor did I hear him. Neither did he drive to our house in a car. He was simply there.

I wasn't the least bit startled or bothered by his appearance, I just assumed either I had not been paying attention, or he somehow snuck up on me. But that was not the only thing about him that I noticed. His uniform somehow looked out of place. Even at age five, I had seen many different kinds of uniforms, as so many of the men in the neighborhood were either active military, or veterans of World War Two or the Korean War. I knew the general cut, design, and colors of the uniforms of the major branches of the U.S. military, and his uniform did not resemble any of them. His was almost impossibly black; I could not see the texture of it, and it had very bright and very eye catching silvery accents and insignia. His uniform practically radiated authority and the right to command. The man also had very deep set eyes, hidden completely by shadows.

I looked at him and said nothing. He looked back at me for a moment, and then started speaking. He addressed me by name, which should have bothered me, as I did not know him. But, at age five, I still assumed adults knew everything, so it was okay with me that he knew my name. He started to speak earnestly; in a way that even I knew meant what he had to tell me was important. I risked a quick look back over my shoulder at my mother, who was in the kitchen at the sink. She glanced briefly at me, but did not seem to notice that man at the door. I turned to look at him again.

He told me that I must remember what he was going to tell me, and that I must tell all the adults in the neighborhood what he said. He stressed that it was very important that I start telling people today what he was going to say, and I must convince people to believe it. He explained that it was so important he would be back to check on me, and to see if the message had been spread. I simply nodded, and he went on.

He explained that before too long, in the coming fall, that it would look like war was coming to the United States, and to the whole world. He said not to worry, because although it would look like the war would come, it would not happen, even though it would get very close. He said people would think that the war would be fought with nuclear weapons, and before I could even say I did not know what those were; he said I should just remember to tell people that no nuclear weapons would be used, and that they would know what that meant.

I started to ask what else I needed to say, but again the man preempted me, and said that was all I needed to tell people for now, and he would tell me more when he came back to check. He looked silently at me for a moment, and then he was gone. I started to get up to go outside, to see if the man was still nearby somewhere, when I heard my mother behind me. She looked out the door for a few seconds, and then walked away, making no mention of having seen the man. I got up and went back to my room, trying to figure out what to do for the rest of the day.

The message the man had given me seemed important, but I had difficulty understanding how I would convince any adult, let alone dozens of them, of what the man had said. What would happen if I didn't do what he said? Maybe he'd forget? Maybe I'd just tell my dad, and he'd make the man stay away? I also wondered why the man chose me, instead of telling an adult. I didn't think I would go around the neighborhood and spread the man's message.

As the afternoon wore on, I got increasingly nervous. Did the man have spies in the neighborhood, watching me, noting I hadn't done anything to give people the message? Maybe I really needed to reconsider, and go out and tell people. Besides, it seemed like something people might believe, and maybe it was even true. I was still thinking about that when my stepfather came home, and dinner started shortly after.

I decided at the end of dinner to start spreading the news. I went to the neighbors closest to our home, and knocked on their doors. When they came, I started right in without introduction, giving just the message, and leaving out the man who had come to my house, other than telling people I had been given this information by a military officer. I was too young to understand the meaning behind the smiling faces, and the spoken gratitude, for the message I gave them. In the early 1960s, people were more polite, and no one was going to tell a five-year-old that he was speaking nonsense, or that he was crazy. Instead, they told his parents. When I got done that evening making my rounds, I went home; the phone was still ringing with neighbors calling about me.

I got screamed at a lot during my childhood and adolescence; likewise, I was beaten an awful lot too. Not because I misbehaved, but because my parents were cruel. That was already old news to me at age five. I had not even bothered to factor in the very look right, they were now more elliptical than round, and they were too big. I got up and walked towards him.

He stood completely still, like a statue, though I could tell, somehow, that his eyes were tracking me. When I got close, I saw that he looked even less human than I had thought. His skin had a peculiar look, rough, like it was composed of small scales. And his color was slightly silvery, and constantly shifting in hue. I watched for a minute, unsure of what this could mean. While I was still thinking about that, he began to speak.

I like his voice this time even less than before. Now it was difficult to understand the words; they tended to blur or get lost in a consistent, shrill, buzzing noise. It got on my nerves, and it made me feel dizzy. I got up to shut the door, but the man shook his slowly, no. I sat back down, and tried to listen.

After a while I realized he was saying the same things, over and over, and waiting a second or two after each repetition, to see if I understood. The message was short, and to the point. After a half-dozen go arounds, I knew what he wanted. I was to go out one more time, and try to convince as many people as possible, that the coming threat of war would not become a war. He was still displeased with my progress; few, if any of the people I had spoken to believed, and more than a few of those I had approached would not listen to me now. He did not say what would happen if I failed again, but I still felt very threatened, and very afraid.

The man appeared to see that I understood, and that I knew what I was supposed to do. And then like the other times, he was just gone. I sat for a moment at the door, and then I got up, and went outside to give people the message.

I was very tired when I got home, as I had made a huge effort to talk to people. I had even stopped people I saw out walking, and flagged some people down in their cars. It didn't matter; no one wanted to hear. I had a reputation by now, and it preceded me. Many of the people I tried to approach at their homes just smiled at me as I approached then waved me away before I could speak. I decided I didn't care anymore if the man came again; I would tell him I was done, and I would not spread his message anymore.

There was trouble when I got home. I was late for dinner, and after being yelled at by my parents, I went to bed without eating. That didn't matter either, as having been out all day in the hot sun had killed my appetite. I spent some time thinking about the man's visit today, and I surprised myself by realizing I had never told my parents about him. Of course, I also never told anyone else about him either, including his visits to my home, other than saying my message came from a military officer.

I slept well, and woke the next morning untroubled. I barely thought of the man that day, and for many days after that. I settled into a routine that didn't include going out to spread the message. Weeks passed with no visits, and I figured the man was done with me. I was wrong.

October had arrived (that's what my parents called it; I still had to grasp the concept of a "month"), and the weather was unusually warm. Even late in the evening, when it would normally be chilly this time of year, it was warm enough to do without a jacket or a sweater. The adults in the neighborhood, including my parents, had become progressively more and more upset about something in a place called Cuba. It involved people called "Russians". I didn't understand a lot of what they talked about, except that there was trouble, and it was getting worse. The adults seemed to think the Russians were going to get us. I wondered if I should go outside and look for the Russians, but I had no idea what they would look like.

The man came one more time, on a Saturday. It was something of a shock, for several reasons. First, I wasn't expecting him. Second, and worse, his appearance had changed again. This time there was almost nothing remotely human about him. He still wore a black uniform, of sorts. But his head and features were grotesquely changed, resembling some kind of insect, with a silvery skin or surface. The features were somewhat blurry, and changed their appearance when I tried to look at him straight on. Still, I could tell he was looking at me through the door, and wanted my attention. I went and stood just inside the screen door, to hear what he would say.

He began to speak, or more precisely, to make noise. I couldn't understand anything of what I heard; it was a mixture of all kinds of harsh sounds, buzzing, gratings, scrapings, etc. The noise made me shiver, yet despite the disturbance it caused, I somehow thought he was trying to tell me something. The noise kept getting louder; I sensed frustration, like he was getting angry that I didn't understand him. Unlike the other visits, he started moving, instead of just standing still, and I saw him reach for the door handle. I slammed the door shut, and ran to hide in the basement.

Eventually, my curiosity got the better of me, and I went upstairs and opened the door. Nothing. He was gone. This time, for good (though I didn't know that at the time). I shut the door, mentally shrugged off today's visit, and went outside.

More time had passed than I thought; it was now early evening. It was a little chilly outside, and the adults in the neighborhood were gathering, talking to each other across the backyard fences. They all looked worried, but there was something else in their faces. It seemed like resignation. I walked around, looking at the people on the other side of the fences, and at my parents. They paid no attention to me. They spoke quietly, not much above a whisper. My hearing being superb, I was able to clearly understand everything they said. They were expecting some kind of attack, and soon. It might destroy the entire country, and cause the deaths of most or all of the people.

As I continued to listen, I realized that the adults were saying their goodbyes to each other, and talking about misunderstandings or arguments they had in the past. Those things were now forgotten, and they were trying to wipe the slates clean. I shook my head at these things. They were all wrong, and I had told them about this before; that is what the man had said. I got ready to tell them one more time.

I started speaking in a fairly loud voice, interrupting them. They first looked at me with irritation, then concern. They started talking amongst themselves, perhaps thinking I wouldn't know they were talking about me, or that I would not understand.

"Why does he think he knows this?"

"Where does he get these things from?"

"What makes him so sure?"

I simply repeated, over and over, what the man hold told me. There would be no war. There would only be the threat of war, and it would seem to be certain, but it would not happen. I told them, again and again, that a man of great importance from the military had come to visit me at home, and he had told me these things. I told them not to worry, and that they could go home, and not think about it.

They simply stood quietly while I spoke the man's message. A few of them spoke briefly, but only to each other, asking how I knew. They did not speak to me. After a time, I stopped talking, and wordlessly went back inside. My parents did not follow me. It was dark now, and I was tired. I took my shoes off, and went to bed with the rest of my clothes on.

The next day was nothing special, though I got in trouble for sleeping with my clothes on. My mother did not speak much to me, though I could tell she was thinking about what I had said yesterday evening. I later heard some of the neighbors talking in their back yard about how things had "simmered down", and "maybe the danger was past". I was not surprised; the man had said so. I went on about my business.

The following days were unremarkable. Nothing much happened, certainly not a war, and nothing was destroyed, nor did I hear anything about people dying. I quickly forgot about the war, the threat of war, the adults' fright, and the man who had come to tell me things. I didn't have room in my mind for much of anything for the long term, and I rarely gave any thought to man or his message after that.

<u>Snapshot</u>

I was going full bore to help fight the war in Vietnam. From Ohio. Cincinnati, precisely. It was 1967, and I was nine years old (ten years old in August). Despite being just five years (or so) older than in 1962, I felt *so* much more worldly and experienced. And I just *knew* the U.S. military needed my help to win that war, so I was happy to oblige. Of course, I wasn't old enough to enlist. But that wasn't going to stop me. I was going to mount a war-making effort from my back yard that would extend my reach to Vietnam, though I wasn't quite sure yet where it was. But world geography would have to wait. The first thing that needed to be done was to develop a weapon.

I thought that would be easy. Now that I was able to read (unlike in 1962, where I barely knew the print version of a few dozen words), I could consult all the knowledge in the marvelous institutions people referred to as libraries. I was amazed at age six to discover there were places where people who didn't know you would let you borrow their books, and trust you to bring them back. I was soon getting library books regularly.

It was from library books that I learned about World War II, and the weapons that had been used in them, especially the exotic and fascinating weapons the Germans had used. I was particularly interested in the V-1 and V-2. I read everything I could find about them at the local library, and also everything they had about model rocketry. I soon exhausted our neighborhood library's store of information on those subjects, so I convinced my grandmother to take me to the much larger library downtown. There I found far more information on rocketry in general, and the V-2 in particular.

I had already decided I would try to build a version of the V-2, as it had more range than the V-1. Even back in World War II, the Nazis had considered the V-2 for even longer ranges, over 300 miles, by adding wings to it, so it could glide back to earth at a shallow angle, instead of just falling back the ground at a steep angle. That particular idea was in a book that was written in German, which I understood not a word of. But the drawings in the book were clear, and I understood the principle without trouble.

Getting started wasn't too much trouble, though I had to work through intermediaries. Local model shops sold rocket kits, and the engines, though you had to be a certain age to buy them. I just gave money to the teen-aged kids in my neighborhood, and had them buy the engines for me. As my needs increased, I then resorted to ordering rocket engines from catalogues, and simply pretending to be older than I was. All they cared about was whether or not the money orders I sent (with an indecipherable signature) would clear. They did, and I got my rocket engines.

It soon became clear to me that I could not wage war from my back yard, or even continue to use my increasingly large test rockets from home. There was a sprawling abandoned farm within walking distance of my home, and I started testing my rockets there. Still, the neighbors could see, and even hear the rockets launch, from blocks away. But no one did anything about it, as long as it was literally not in my back yard (or theirs).

I had to develop a way to know how far my rockets traveled, and where they landed. I also had to make as certain as possible that when they landed, they would not cause any damage. So, I made them out of light materials; balsa wood for the fins and wings, cardboard tubes for the bodies. The heaviest parts were the engines, which were just very thick pressed cardboard tubes with propellant inside. Still, as I made larger and larger rockets, with more and more engines and stages, they packed quite a punch at launch. The amounts of flame, smoke, and noise were spectacular, and if one of the larger rockets veered off course early and accelerated into a house, car, or person, the results could be disastrous. I thought the possibility of those things happening as remote, and as acceptable risks.

It was possible to estimate, crudely, how high my rockets were going. After much work, my largest rockets were peaking at altitudes miles up. I then worked on the problem of getting them to glide as long as possible, for the greatest range. That wasn't too hard, once I figured out how to tell where the rockets were landing. I simply placed on address label on each rocket, with my address, and postage stamps inside an insulated compartment in the rocket's tube. The address label stated that "if found, use the stamps inside the tube for postage, and mail to the address on the label." The postmarks on the tubes when they came back through the Post Office told me, roughly, where the rockets landed. My best efforts got some of them to Dayton, Ohio, about 40 miles from where I lived.

It was at about that time that trouble began to occur. Some of the neighbors complained to my parents about my "missile base". They did not like the noise of the rockets launching, and as my efforts became steadily grander, they become more and more afraid something disastrous would happen. The neighbors were also alarmed by the "warlike" appearance of the rockets; I painted them black, adding skulls and crossbones, giving them a very ominous look. I'm sure some of my neighbors were afraid I would wage war on them.

From the increasingly rising discomfort my neighbors had with me came pleas for help from the local law enforcement. I eventually noticed the police watching my rocket launches, while they were parked nearby in their cars. They studied my activities with unfriendly stares. I stared back, and acknowledged their attentions with a shrug. I did not care. I knew I would succeed, no matter what was arrayed against me.

For several months I continued to launch rockets from the abandoned farm. The rockets got larger and larger, the amount of noise and flames at launch got bigger and bigger, and the appearance of the rockets looked more and more menacing. I was exalted at the results, literally bursting with pride that *I* did that, when one of my missiles took flight. I felt like I held the hammer of God, and that I personally had been chosen to strike our enemies.

The police did nothing but watch for the longest time. They never once spoke to me. I didn't care; I had nothing to say to them. And I couldn't imagine they had anything interesting to say to me. After a while they stopped coming to watch me. I thought that might be the end of it, but I was wrong.

One day two men dressed in military uniforms came to our house (they were really there, as my mother saw them too). They asked to speak to me, after introducing themselves to my mother. They sat down with both of us in the living room, and explained very patiently that while my efforts in helping to fight the war in Vietnam were noble, that the U.S. military could handle things on their own. They also suggested that I no longer conduct experiments in rocketry. I accepted their recommendations without question, and without reservation. While I regretted not being able to further my rocketry to the point that I could reach Vietnam, I decided to let the adults handle the business of making war.

<u>Snapshot</u>

In the summer of 1966, I was well aware of the "race riots" that were erupting across the country. There had been some in the city I lived in, a normally unremarkable, mid-size Midwestern population of about 350,000 people. Some nights I could stand in the back yard, and see the orange reddish glow on the horizon from the parts of the city that were burning. Even as a child, I realized the gravity of the situation. People needed to protect themselves from the violence and the destruction that was raging around them.

I thought the solution was obvious; you needed to get a gun. More precisely, *I* needed to get a gun. Even though I was just a child, I was well aware of the curfews that had been imposed repeatedly throughout the city, lasting from 6:00 P.M. until 6:00 A.M. the next day. Being outside of your home without a good reason meant arrest. I also saw daily the frantic carloads of men trying to get home from work before the hardware stores closed, hoping to get the last boxes of shotgun shells or pistol rounds.

My family owned no guns, though my grandparents did. Their relatives were hunters, woodsmen, and farmers, and they were well acquainted with guns, and had an ample supply of both long guns and side arms. Yes, back then in the 1960s, it was easy for adults to buy guns. But, as a child, what to do?

I decided to use the mail order method. Yes, in that prehistoric time, you could mail order a gun, just about any kind of gun. You could even order a fully automatic weapon, like a machine gun. For some kinds of guns, you only needed to fill out an order card, and send the money. The gun would come, completely legally, through the Post Office. That appealed to me, as no one would check, as long as they were paid.

I looked through a stack of gun company ads in magazines, and also gun catalogues. I made the decision to buy a .38-caliber nickel-plated revolver. It was a reasonably compact gun that could easily be carried in a pocket, but had large enough rounds to cause serious damage at close range.

I had money saved from doing chores, from my allowance, gifts, and foraging for coins people dropped in public places. Despite that, could I afford to buy a gun? Easily, as the gun I picked (brand new) didn't even cost $20. Guns back then were incredibly cheap, and the one I chose was not a poorly make "knock off"; it was from a well-known manufacturer. Payment was not a problem, either. I went to a local convenience store and purchased a money order. The signature I put to it before mailing it was an illegible scribble.

I placed the order for the gun, including a card stating I was 25 years old (yes, I lied). I waited, and about 6 weeks later, a small box arrived on our front porch. I made sure to intercept it before my mother saw it. I unwrapped the box, securely packed inside was the gun. It looked just like the picture. I hid the gun in my closet, underneath a pile of winter clothing and board games, while I thought about what to do with it.

I didn't need to worry about ammunition. While I could have ordered bullets when I ordered the gun, I didn't. My grandfather had ammunition that would work in the gun I purchased. It would be a simple matter to "borrow" some from my grandfather's storage the next time I went to my grandparents' house. But in some ways that didn't solve anything. I still needed to decide how I was going to use a loaded gun when the time came to use it.

I had some experience with guns already; some of our relatives hunted regularly, and they had taught me how to use rifles and pistols. But, shooting at targets and animals was different than shooting at people, at least in theory. My actual feelings on the matter were different; if I needed to use that gun to protect myself, a human target would be no different than a paper target. I'd feel no guilt at gunning someone down who was trying to hurt or to kill me. But even as a child, I knew others (adults) would not necessarily see it that way. So I decided to discuss it with my grandfather.

I waited until one day my parents were gone, then I phoned my grandparents, telling them I needed them to come over, as I had something to show them. Though they were curious about what it was, I said it was a surprise. When they arrived, I had the box with the gun waiting in the living room. I explained briefly what I had done, and showed them the gun. My grandmother looked moderately shocked, while my grandfather did not show much of a reaction.

My grandfather asked me why I had purchased the gun, and I told him about using it for self-defense during the race riots I thought were coming. He thought about my explanation for a minute, and only said "oh". He then asked for the gun, which I gave him. I never saw the gun again, and I never thought much more about it. As it turned out, I never needed the gun for the current disturbances. Well, so much for planning.

Snapshot

It was only about a year after the end of my rocketry efforts that I had another unusual, and unique, experience. This time, I had ample adult participation, though it did not help resolve the mystery any better.

There was an abandoned family farm less than a mile from where I lived. Despite the ramshackle nature of some of the buildings, it was a lovely place, with the remains of an orchard, pasturelands, and a stream with a waterfall, a house, and a barn. It was the barn that was the center of interest.

My friends and I had explored the farm thoroughly, and knew it well. The barn had a spacious basement, and in it were the hulks of three cars from the 1950s. I was fascinated by the ornate and garish styling of the cars, and being a child, I naively thought I could figure out how to get the cars running. However, the electric lighting in the basement had long failed, and it was hard to see the detail in the cars. Even in the daytime, the light was fairly dim. So, I took to bringing flashlights to the barn.

One day while I was fooling around in the basement, I lost track of time. When I finally noticed, it was darker outside than I would have liked. While I didn't have far to walk home, I didn't like being in the barn near dark. I switched the flashlights on and walked out. I almost immediately noticed when I got outside that there was no "night noise"; no sounds from crickets or cicadas, no barking from the neighbors' dogs, and no owls hooting.

While walking around the barn I shined the flashlight into an open door at ground level, and stopped. I stared for a moment, trying to make sense of what I saw, and making sure I actually saw what I thought I saw. It appeared the beam of the flashlight stopped dead at the open doorway; I was certain the doorframe didn't even have a door to block the light. I walked right up to the doorway, holding the light on it. While the frame was illuminated by the beam, the opening was completely dark; I could see nothing.

I set the flashlight down on the ground, pointing towards the doorway. I picked up a rock, and tossed it in. The rock "disappeared" when it reached the boundary of the doorway, but a second later I heard it hit the floor inside. I still couldn't see it, or anything else in the room. While I should have been dumbfounded, I was actually only moderately curious. How did this work? I wondered briefly how to answer this question.

Despite my curiosity, I wasn't interested in walking through the doorway, even with the flashlight. What was going on in there? There must be some other way to figure this out without going in. I thought about that for a moment, and realized I had been in this room several days ago, during the daylight, and though the lighting inside was fairly dim, I had no trouble finding my way around. Well, that meant that light was able to get into the room that day, at least sunlight. Something didn't seem to add up here.

I decided to let my discovery go for another day, maybe tomorrow. I walked home slowly, thinking about the dark room that would not let light in (or did the room eat light?). My thoughts went round and round on this point until I got home. I thought about it even more after I got ready for bed, and lay down and tried to sleep.

The next day I woke up with a modest plan in mind. I'd go back to the farmhouse and see what the room looked like in the daylight. Then I could go from there. I wasn't the least bit worried about what I would find, and I was actually interested in what would happen. I got dressed quickly, and was out the door without stopping for breakfast. Besides bringing the flashlight with me, I also brought some firecrackers, and some matches.

When I reached the farmhouse I went to the doorway that had defied my flashlight beam the previous evening. Despite the sun shining directly onto that side of the barn, the doorway was jet black; I could not see into the room. I decided to try an experiment. I approached the doorway. I walked up to it, and held on to the doorframe with one hand, while stepping through as far as possible without letting go.

As soon as I stepped across the threshold into the room, everything went pitch black. I fought my natural reaction to turn and run away, and instead waited for my eyes to dark adapt. They didn't. I could see nothing, no matter how long I waited. I had the flashlight with me, and I turned it on. Nothing. No light came out, or did it?

I backed out a few steps until I was outside again, and looked at the flashlight. The bulb was lit, and I could see the light it cast on the ground, in the shadow cast by the barn. I held the flashlight out in front of me, reaching past the doorframe into the room. There was nothing, it was as if the room had swallowed up the light. It also looked like my arm had been cut off just above the elbow. I withdrew my arm from the room and turned the flashlight off. I had my whole arm back.

The next step was very clear; I was going to use the fire crackers. They were in a strip of about forty. I picked a few of them out of the strip, making sure they had long fuses. I got a book of matches from my shirt pocket, lit one of the firecrackers, and tossed it through the doorway. The firecracker disappeared as soon as it crossed the threshold, though I heard it hit the floor. A few seconds later, I heard the detonation. It was loud, but I didn't even see the hint of a flash. A moment later the smoke from the explosion drifted out of the doorway into the sunlight.

I decided to go for broke. I got the whole strip of firecrackers out of my pocket, and straightened the fuse that would start the entire chain of firecrackers exploding. I lit the fuse carefully, and tossed it through the doorway. A few seconds later, the firecrackers began exploding, with the entire strip lasting about 15 seconds. I never saw a hint of light from the strip of firecrackers; I only heard them go off. For several minutes after the last of them exploded, smoke drifted out of the doorway. Then, silence.

I wasn't quite sure what to do at this point to solve the riddle of the room that ate light. I didn't begin to understand how this could be possible. I still had ideas, though. Could a bright enough light penetrate the darkness in the room? What would happen if the barn eventually collapsed, or was torn down? Would there still be a dark space that could not be illuminated, out in the open? I decided to enlist some adults to help.

As I walked home, I considered who I would ask. The logical choice would be someone in the neighborhood who had military experience, and there were plenty of people like that. Just on our block there was a healthy sprinkling of veterans from World War Two, the Korean War, and the Vietnam Conflict. These were people who were used to dealing with unusual situations, and coming up with solutions to problems on the fly. They were also hard-headed, and most of them were combat experienced, so they weren't easily rattled. They were just the choice for this situation.

I thought about who to ask for the next several days, and narrowed it down to several World War Two veterans, including a U.S. Marine, and an army veteran with two tours of duty in Vietnam. I rehearsed mentally what I would say to them; how I would explain what I found, what I had done, and what I would like them to do. When I approached them, it was actually much easier to convince them to help than I thought. Each one of them listened to me thoughtfully and silently, only speaking to ask probing questions. At the end of my account, each man looked at me very seriously, before saying he would help.

I am certain the men I spoke to in turn spoke to each other afterwards, though they did not tell me what had been said. One of them called me at home several days later, and said they were going to take a look at the room in the barn, though they thought it best I not be present. I didn't object much, as I had already decided it was time to hand this venture over to adult intervention. They did promise they would let me know what they found when they were done. I waited.

About a week later I got another phone call from one of the men I had spoken to, though it was a different person than the one who had called before. He said that they were going to make their last attempt tonight to light up the room in the barn. He also said that I could come, but I should wait for one of the men I had spoken to earlier to come and get me. The seriousness of his tone made it clear to me that I should cooperate. I did.

I waited outside after dinner for someone to come; I didn't know who it would be. About dusk a car I hadn't seen before pulled up at the curb; the driver motioned me over. I walked to the car and got in; no questions asked. The driver and I didn't exchange a word on the short drive to the farmhouse. We parked on the street near the property where the barn was. The driver got out, and I followed him to the barn. It was dark by then, but I could still see there were cars parked on the grass near the barn. There were deep ruts and tire tread marks where people had driven their cars off the street through a clear section in the woods to get to the barn. Their headlights were on, illuminating the barn and the doorway to the room. Some of the cars had spotlights, and they were on, trained towards the doorway.

Amazingly, I saw that they had rented a powerful searchlight, the kind you often saw in the 1960s, mounted on a flatbed truck, shining into the night sky to advertise a new business. It had been manhandled onto the property behind the barn, and it was pointing at the doorway, though the searchlight had not been turned on yet.

My eyes had adapted to the dark, and I could see there were about a dozen men outside the back of the barn. They were clustered in small groups, talking in low tones. Once in a while one of them would glance at the doorway, where the cars' headlights and spotlights were trained. I could see that the doorway was as black as ink; nothing of the light reaching the door entered or illuminated the interior.

I felt a hand on my shoulder. I looked, and recognized the man who had brought me here. He beckoned for me to follow him. I did. I walked a short distance to where the searchlight was. The other men were gathered around it. One of them turned a key on what looked like a generator, and it started running. Some of the men moved the searchlight so that it pointed at the doorway, and then a blindingly white beam of light appeared.

The amount of light striking the barn was overwhelmingly dazzling, but it may as well have been a match sputtering in the dark, as the doorway to the room was jet black. The light reflected from the barn wall was too bright too look at directly, but the doorway remained stubbornly dark. One of the men made as if to walk through the doorway, but the others waved him back. I had no bold compulsions to walk through that door.

The men adjusted the beam of the searchlight, moving up and down, and from side to side, a bit. It made no difference. After a few more minutes, they turned the generator off. The car headlights and spotlights were still on, but people began to turn them off. In another ten minutes the only light came from a few flashlights, and the stars overhead. My eyes were dark adapting by then, and I could see people getting ready to leave. Some of them were moving the searchlight to a small flatbed trailer I hadn't noticed before; others were getting in their cars and starting them up.

I started to walk away, intending to walk home on my own, but one of the men in the group tapped me on the shoulder, and then spoke.

"You don't have to worry about what's going to happen after tonight. It's taken care of".

I wondered what "taken care of" meant, but I decided not to ask. The man looked at me to make sure I understood, and when I said nothing else, he motioned for me to follow him to his car. I got in; the ride home was short and quiet.

In the days following that night, I resisted the urge to visit the barn as long as I could. After a couple of weeks, I gave in to my curiosity, and walked to the barn on a Saturday. At least, I tried to walk to the barn. When I got there, I saw the barn was no longer there. It had been torn down, with only the concrete floor remaining, with various bits of scrap lumber.

I walked around the border of the floor, and then walked onto it, crossing where I guessed the perpetually dark room had been. It was as completely sunlit as any other part of the floor, and looked completely ordinary. I spent another few moments looking around; there was no evidence of the former light-destroying characteristics of the room that had been there. For some reason I wasn't surprised; I assumed the men who had been there that night with the searchlight were responsible for the demolition of the barn. I spent a few more moments looking at the remains of the barn, and then I left. I never returned, and I never heard any more about it.

<u>Snapshot</u>

There are other notable instances of remarkable events in my life that are worth cataloging. They key word is notable. All of the events were notable, though not all of them were remarkable, or monumental. So, this event was one of the notable ones.

While I was in my early teens, that was long enough ago that all kinds of products that were for children and sold then, would not be remotely allowed for sale now, because of safety concerns. One of those products was fluorescent paint; it could be put on many different things, including your own body. It was water soluble, and supposedly non-toxic. I didn't really care about that, as I didn't intend to use it on myself.

The paint could be applied with an ordinary artist's brush, like you would use for paint-by-numbers paintings, or for model building. It fluoresced well enough, as I had tested it on various items; painting toys, models, and even the fence in the back yard, and seeing how well they glowed at night. The light given off by the paint was fairly bright, visible at a fair distance, and appearing a sickly yellow-green. It would certainly do for what I intended.

Perhaps one would think I would paint myself, and go creeping around the neighborhood at night to frighten people. But, no, I had something much better in mind. I'd paint our dog with the glowing paint, and turn him loose at night. While we had a cat, they were too fastidious about their grooming to leave the paint on their fur. A cat would try to lick it off, while a dog wouldn't care.

Our dog was a medium-sized mixed breed; half Collie and half German-shepherd, weighing about 70 pounds. He liked nocturnal hours, and was active at night. Perfect. One day I used several bottles of the fluorescent paint on him, and painted him to look like a skeleton. I was able to tell how he would look after I finished painting, because I put him in the basement with the lights off, and the windows shaded. He had a ghastly appearance, especially when he was moving. He looked like a glowing animal skeleton; the worst part was when he faced you, with the glowing outline of the skull and the empty eye sockets.

Why did I go to all this trouble? My neighbors were inconsiderate idiots, who often came past our house late at night on the way home from work, revving their engines blowing their horns, and cranking up their radios. They also tended to party until the early hours of the morning, with loud music and lots of yelling. It was time to address these problems in the worst way possible.

Late one Friday evening I painted the dog, and after allowing time for the paint to dry, I let him loose. There were not many streetlights on our block to spoil the illusion, so I had every reason to believe he would be noticed by people driving through. (I had not made the obvious connection that he would also be noticed by people in their houses; that would factor in to the results later.) I watched for a few minutes after letting the dog go, but he had already run out of sight. I sat down on the floor near the living room window and waited, but I heard and saw nothing other than ordinary neighborhood night activity and noises. I got up and went upstairs to my bedroom.

I had settled in to reading a book in my bed for almost an hour, before I heard the first eruptions of panic in the night. I wasn't sure at first, but I thought I heard a sudden burst of high-pitched screaming, followed by a man's shouting. I heard a door slam, and then I heard nothing. I waited, listening intently, sometimes hearing faint sounds at a distance that might be from disturbances.

I was just about ready to give up and go back to reading when I heard another loud explosion of noises. I heard the shrieking of car tires as someone panic braked to a stop, joined by bellowed curses and threats. Several car doors slammed, and I heard people shouting in alarmed voices. I didn't hear anything after that for several minutes, and then I heard the noise of a car peeling out, and horns blowing. I didn't think that this burst of noise was coincidentally following the earlier eruption. I decided to go back down to the living room and watch, to see if I was right. I was.

After about twenty minutes of watching from the darkened living room, I saw the dog across the street, running through a neighbor's front yard. Several people were chasing him, and throwing things at him. He seemed to think it was a game, doubling back and barking at the people, who ran away. He watched them for a minute, and then decided to run across the street, just in time to cross the path of an oncoming car. The driver noticed the glowing dog skeleton coming across the lawn and into the street, and stomped on the brakes, bringing the car to a tire-smoking halt. Without missing a beat, he wrenched the car around into a U-turn, driving up over the curb and tearing up the grass in the neighbor's front yard. The man gunned the engine, gaining the street again, and accelerating rapidly into the dark.

I decided enough damage had been done for the night, and went outside to get the dog in. However, he didn't want to come in yet, and ignored my calls. When I tried to go get him to bring in by force, he ran away. Well, I guess I'd wait him out, looking for him to return home when he was done. As I walked back to the house, someone in home where I was cutting across the yard opened a window and leaned out. He yelled "do you know what that thing is?". I pretended not to hear him. I got back home and went inside.

For the next several hours I heard a cacophony of noises, from startled yells to what I thought were gunshots. Once or twice the dog came close enough to our house for me to see him briefly. The glowing skeleton's appearance was getting a bit ragged; I assumed that came from the dog running through underbrush or crawling under fences. At about 3:00 A.M., things seemed to be winding down. I hadn't heard any unusual noises in about the last hour.

Our dog sauntered over from across the street, looking tired. I couldn't imagine all the places he might have been, but I was sure he'd run across most, or even all, of our neighbors. I let him in, got the glowing paint off him, and went to bed. The aftermath of the night's ventures was a much quieter neighborhood for the next several weeks. I felt the effort was well worth it.

Snapshot

I was never involved with the occult or the paranormal; I never practiced any rituals to summon demons, communicate with the dead, or cast spells. While I tried an Ouija board a few times, I never got anything but gibberish. Still, the house I lived in gave me very bad feelings at times. Sometimes when I was in the basement I was overwhelmed with feelings of dread and fright. The feelings were so strong at times I had to go upstairs. At other times I would have those feelings when I was on the second floor in my bedroom. It was always when I was alone in the house.

It could be argued that I was the victim of nothing more than an overactive imagination (which I had). However, if that was the case, I likely would have those feelings routinely, not just in my house, not just in certain rooms, and more often than once in a while. Again, since there were nothing more than feelings, maybe nothing was really happening. However, there came a day when something happened to completely convince me that some malignant force was operating in our house.

One day the family I was living with (I was adopted) went out that evening, and left me at home. I had not wished to make the trip to where they were going, and I was quite happy to stay at home by myself. I would have an entire three-day weekend alone in the house. I wasn't planning to throw a party (I wasn't the party type); I planned to watch movies on TV late at night, and read some science fiction. It was actually looking to be a pretty good holiday weekend.

The first day (Friday) I was alone, I was lazing on the couch in the living room, reading a magazine, when something started to bother me. I felt like someone else was in the house with me, though there was no reason for that to be true; besides the cat, who was sitting on the windowsill in the living room, no other living thing was in the house. Still, I couldn't shake the feeling. I tried concentrating on my reading, but I couldn't. I finally put the magazine aside, and got up to walk around the house.

I had no idea what I was looking for, other than anything that seemed out of place. As I walked through the living room, and past the doorway to the stairs going to the second floor, I noticed the lights in one of the second floor bedrooms were on. Hadn't I turned them off earlier today? The thought nagged at me. I slowly climbed the stairs, feeling a little anxious. I got to the second floor landing, just outside the bedroom doorway, and stopped. I didn't want to go in. Why?

I hesitated for a moment, and then resolutely strode into the room. I saw nothing amiss. Simply, the ceiling lights in the room were on. Before I turned the lights off, I checked the clothes closet, and nothing but the usual jumble of clothes and toys were in there. I walked out of the room, resisting the strong urge to look back, and turned the lights off on the way out. I walked back downstairs, already feeling relief.

I turned the TV on, and began to watch the first movie I found, something about a man building a plantation in Africa. I wasn't that interested in the movie, and my attention wandered. I got an unsettling feeling that something was wrong again. I didn't want to get up and look, but I did. I walked to the doorway to the second floor, and looked up to the second floor landing; the lights in the bedroom were on again. Damn it! I knew good and well I turned those lights off a little while ago, and now they were back on.

How could that be? Did I go back and turn them on, forgetting I had done so? Did I just think I'd turned them off, when I actually didn't? I didn't consider either of those possibilities to be even remotely likely. Well, what then? For some reason I was in no hurry to find out what was going on, but I was not able to forget about it, either. I fumed for a moment at the bottom of the stairs, and then slowly climbed up.

I listened very intently, walking as quietly as possible. I heard nothing. I reached the landing, and looked in the bedroom. The overhead lights were on again, but nothing else seemed to have changed. I took some extremely reluctant steps into the bedroom, and looked around. I still saw nothing amiss, but I sure as hell could not explain how those lights were on. They were very ordinary lights controlled by the ubiquitous type toggle switches, simply on, or off. You had to flip them up to turn them on, and flip them down to turn them off. I looked around once more, and turned the lights off. I left the room and went downstairs.

I spent the next thirty minutes or so outside, trying to read a book in the failing evening light. I could have stayed out longer by turning on the porch light, but somehow

I knew I would have to go back inside. I also knew what I would find, so why did I need to look? Maybe I was a glutton for punishment. I put the book down, and went inside.

I decided to do things differently this time. I went into the kitchen, and cut a piece of tape off the roll on the counter. I held it in one hand; as I got to the stairway entrance, I could tell the lights were on again. I took a deep breath, closed my eyes, and yelled as loud as I could, "the lights are off!!" I counted to three, and opened my eyes. The lights were still on. I started climbing, taking the stairs one leaden step at a time. I felt very strongly like I was being watched, but that was completely irrational. I went upstairs anyway.

When I got to the landing I walked right in to the bedroom. I looked around very carefully, and saw nothing amiss. The overhead lights burned brightly. Well, we'll just see about that, I thought. I flipped the switches off, and then taped them down. I walked downstairs confidently, thinking the problem solved.

I tried watching television for an hour or so, flipping through the channels over and over, not settling on anything. During this time the sun set, adding to my growing sense that I was trapped inside the house. That was simply my imagination working overtime. But the next thought was simple, and obvious. How did I know what was real? All I had to do was check if the lights were still off. So, I got up and looked. They weren't. They were on.

I almost expected to have a violent reaction to this, but I didn't. I almost didn't care; it's like I expected it. I looked up the stairs at the brightly burning lights. On the steps in front of me was the piece of tape I used to tape the light switches in the off position. Though there was no logical reason for it to have been removed, and to be there on the steps, I was not surprised. Perhaps I was fatalistic, in some way. I walked up the stairs, thinking about not much at all, only a little concerned about what I might find.

I reached the landing and walked resolutely into the bedroom. I was hyper alert, and extremely nervous. I slowly scanned the room several times, and still saw nothing unusual or out of place. As I was looking through the room for the third time, I noticed a small wooden model ship on one of the dressers. Odd that I hadn't noticed it before, but I knew it was supposed to be in the room. I looked closer, and saw that the ship's rigging was moving slightly, like from a light breeze. But there was no breeze in that room; there were no fans, and the windows were closed. I looked again, and the rigging was still moving. I decided to leave.

I had the urge to run, but I resisted, and walked at a slow, steady pace towards the doorway. As I reached it, I heard a noise behind me, and stopped to look. The wooden model ship was moving across the dresser, and I watched it, both horrified and fascinated. As I watched, it moved towards the edge of the dresser, and fell over it onto the floor with a loud clatter. My nerve broke, and I turned to run, reaching reflexively towards the light switches to turn them off. My hand never reached them; with about a foot to go before my fingers touched the switches, they flipped from on to off by themselves.

I screamed as if the dead were rising, and ran downstairs and out the front door at lightning speed. I spent the rest of the night outside, not daring to go back in. I slept a few hours on the patio in the back yard; otherwise I sat outside, or paced nervously in the back yard. I did not go back in the house until well after sunup, when the sun was clearly above the horizon, and the sunlight was nice and bright. When I finally went inside, I felt completely at ease. And, the lights were still off.

When my family returned from their vacation several days later, the lights upstairs were still behaving normally, and they did so afterwards. There was never another incident like those during my family's absence. And I never mentioned any of it to them.

<u>Snapshot</u>

One summer my family went to Canada on a camping trip. We drove for several days, towing a fold-up camper with us. When we got to Canada, we stayed at a campground that had fairly typical facilities. However, one way in which it differed from those in the U.S. we had stayed at was the immense and lush forest that surrounded the campground. It was an almost impossibly dense jungle of trees of all sizes, from young saplings to gigantic older trees.

I spent some time exploring the outer edges of the forest during the daytime, but I did not go deeper. It would have been very easy to get lost, and I did not wish to take that risk. It was also difficult to navigate the forest, as there were no paths through it. The nearest path didn't go through the forest; it skirted the edge, and went around the campground's borders. The branches from the larger trees hung over the path, giving it a semi-enclosed appearance with a leafy canopy. The shade it gave during the day was nice, but at night the overhanging branches were uncomfortable, making me feel closed in.

One day while trying to kill time, I looked in the glove box of the car we drove on the trip. I was only mildly surprised to find a gun in there. I recognized the gun almost immediately, it was my grandfather's. I remembered my mother discussing with him several months ago that they were thinking of getting a gun for the house. So, he must have given them the gun one time we were visiting; they put it in the glovebox before going home, and forgot it was in there.

The gun was an antique, but fully functional; it was a five-shot nickel-plated revolver manufactured in the 1890s. It was chambered for .38-caliber rounds; not exactly a hand-held howitzer or cannon, but it would do for home defense. I unlocked the gun's cylinder and popped it out of the frame. Christ, it was loaded!! All five chambers had rounds in them! I couldn't believe my parents had left a loaded gun in the car, but there it was. I pushed the cylinder back in the frame, and locked it in. I held the gun in my hand for a moment while I thought.

I decided to hide the gun in the camper, in one of the small stowage compartments we never used. That would give me time to figure out what to do with the gun later. Part of my mind chimed in with the thought that I should tell my parents now I had found the gun, and it was loaded. But for some reason, it seemed vital that I not tell, and keep the gun's location a secret. I felt like I needed that gun for something, but I had no idea what. I hid the gun, and went on with my day.

We spent most of the day and the evening away from the camp site, visiting tourist attractions, and a few restaurants, getting back just a little before nightfall. My parents wanted to make a fire in the fire pit behind our camper, but there was no wood. It fell to me to find some. I went out on the path that marked the edge of the forest, and looked for branches that had fallen from the overhanging trees. The work went slowly, in part because there was little artificial lighting along the path, and I had to rely on light from peoples' campers, and a flashlight I brought. I spent the next several hours collecting kindling, and bringing it back to our campsite. I judged that I had enough near midnight.

The time bothered me, as I was somewhat superstitious. Midnight was the wrong time to be out at night, as it was the witching hour, when evil was supposed to be active and walking abroad. I had brought the gun with me, and I touched it to be sure it was still in my pants' pocket. I took some comfort in its presence, though I wasn't sure what good a gun would be against black magic.

I started walking back towards our campsite, carrying the last batch of wood. It was quiet; most of the people in the campground had gone to bed, and there was no breeze to rustle the trees' branches. I turned the flashlight off, as I could actually see better in some ways without it. There was a little light from the half-full moon, so I could see the path without much trouble. Still, I walked cautiously, not wanting to stumble over something in the shadows.

I was about to pass under a particularly large overhang of branches when I heard a noise above me, just ahead. Something was rustling in the branches overhanging the path. I stopped dead in my tracks, too frightened to move another step. The noise subsided, and I started to persuade myself to keep going, when something fell out of the tree branches. It landed about five to six feet in front of me with a fairly loud thud.

I couldn't quite understand what I was looking at; it appeared to be about the size and shape of a small child, but I couldn't see it clearly, only the general outline and appearance. For a few seconds my mind tried to rationalize it as something ordinary, and failed. My rationalizations ceased when whatever it was stood, and displayed at least four ropy arms, which began lashing the dirt in front of it, making loud "thwacking" noises. My breath caught in my throat, and I felt panic rising in me.

Without thinking I pulled the revolver from my pocket, and frantically squeezed the trigger, over and over. The gun blasts sounded shockingly loud, though I knew from experience the reports were more like small firecrackers. Whatever it was that I was shooting at was at point blank range, and I did not miss. I saw the thing jerk with the impact of the bullets, and tumble backwards. I felt momentary relief, only to be frightened once more when it got back up. I squeezed the trigger again, but the hammer only fell on empty shells.

Whatever it was had been hurt, and it hopped/limped slowly into the forest. I watched it go, having no desire whatsoever to either follow it or to stop it. It disappeared quietly, with barely a rustle of foliage to mark its passage. I stood there, completely still, for a few moments, wondering if it would come back, or if someone who had heard the gunshots would come to investigate. Neither happened. I took a deep breath, put the gun back in my pocket, and started walking slowly. I listened intently, but I heard nothing. I began to walk faster, trying to put as much distance between me and the thing as quickly as possible.

It wasn't long before I reached our camper. I saw that my family had already started a fire with the wood I brought. They were sitting around it, oblivious to what had happened. I watched the fire for a minute, and then I went to put the gun in its hiding place. I then took off my clothes, and went to bed. I fell asleep in minutes.

The next morning came quickly, but I was able to get dressed quickly after waking. My first order of business was to go back to the place on the trail where I had fired the gun. I wanted to run, but I forced myself to walk. I soon found the spot where I had been frightened by…..something. The dirt was disturbed where the thing had lashed it, and I thought I could see a few places where the bullets had struck the ground. There were also small dried puddles of something sticky, which had a bad odor. I looked for a few minutes more, and then I walked back to the camper. I wasn't the least bit tempted to enter the wood to see whatever it was might be lying in there dead. I never said anything to anyone about the experience, and I never heard anything about it. In time, I forgot about, except for a rare remembrance.

<u>Snapshot</u>

Probably every male child has a fascination at some point with starting fires. And the number of fires is only exceeded by the creativity in deciding what to burn. Like most male children, I wanted to see mayhem and destruction on an industrial scale. But how was that to be arranged? I decided to burn and destroy scale models of things, instead of full-sized objects. So, my efforts were directed at bags of plastic army soldiers, model planes, model ships and submarines. My imagination knew no bounds, and it was satisfied by my disciplined and steadfast perseverance in creating things to destroy by fire.

I originally planned and executed these events solo. These were not the kinds of things you invited people to (especially adults, as they'd try to stop you), and I was much happier to be alone to enjoy the events by myself. My first efforts were with dozens of green plastic army men; you could get a bag of a hundred of them for three dollars. I'd take them out to a bare patch in the nearby woods, set them up, and then soak the ground they stood on with charcoal lighter fluid. One match was all it took to set the soldiers ablaze, and it was fascinating to watch the flames literally come up out of the ground to consume them. They melted slowly, twisting into grotesque shapes, before catching fire. When it was all over there was just a blackened patch of earth, with bubbling liquid plastic. It was great!!

I tired of burning collections of soldiers, and looked for something else. My mind soon provided an answer. Simply use my model-building skills to make biplanes, ships, and submarines. Planes going down in flames would be a great sight, while ships burning and going under would be entertaining. And what of the submarines? They could be packed with firecrackers with long fuses, which would detonate when the submarines were underwater. Now I had a plan, I made it happen.

Several weeks of feverish activity passed. I spent all of my available time building several large model biplanes, the type with a balsa wood frame and tissue "canvas". They each had a wingspan of over two feet. I took them to the nearby woods where there was a small, rocky peak that was about four stories tall. I wound the planes up (they had rubber band "motors"), soaked them in charcoal lighter fluid, lit them with a match, and let them go.

The scale models of the World War One fighters made spectacular flaming pathways in the skies, with great billows of smoke. None of the flights lasted more than a few minutes, and the planes' death spirals were ended by collisions with trees or the earth. It never occurred to me that the flaming planes could start a forest fire, and it never happened. But, while burning things was great, exploding things was even better, as the violence of the destruction was much greater. I went to phase two.

I went back to model building, but this time it was model ships and submarines. I built the larger ships, usually aircraft carriers. In the nearby forest was a stream with a waterfall which fed into a small pond. It was there I brought my ships. I packed them with small firecrackers, and lit one end of the vessels, while pushing them gently towards the center of the pond. The ships would usually detonate after floating for just a few minutes, producing a multicolored shower of parts, before the remains of the hulls sank beneath the surface. To this day the remains of several dozen model vessels are on the bottom of that pond.

Watching (miniature) aircraft carriers, battleships, cruisers and destroyers descend into the depths was great fun, but what could possibly be better? I soon found that answer; I would build model submarines that would actually submerge, and detonate them under water. Again, I went back to model building. I had the first two submarines ready in three weeks. These were working model submarines that would dive and resurface automatically. The mechanisms were not very complicated, though there was some risk that a submarine might dive too deep, and not resurface. I didn't care about that, as I didn't expect the submarines to come back anyway.

Again, I took both submarines to the pond I had taken the model surface vessels to. I had enough firecrackers in both submarines to blow them apart. While the submarines could submerge quickly, I had a lengthy fuse for the firecrackers, so there was time for the submarines to dive deeply (maybe eight to ten feet down) before detonating. I sent both submarines on their way, watching them submerge after lighting the fuses. I waited tensely, wondering if they would explode, or if nothing would happen. I was soon rewarded with a pair of bright flashes, almost at the same time, briefly illuminating a portion of the pond's bottom with some fish swimming nearby. A small disturbance roiled the surface of the pond a moment later.

I watched for a little while, but nothing else happened. While it was satisfying, it was over too soon. I thought about all the work I had done to make the two submarines, versus the brief time I spent watching them destroyed. I got up and slowly walked home, wondering if there was something more entertaining to do, while requiring less work. I thought about it even more after I got home. It was not long after that I decided to try other avenues for my creative energies.

Snapshot

A little knowledge is a dangerous thing. That was one of the expressions I heard when I was a child in the 1960s. That, coupled with my brief life span, and equally limited knowledge about the world, conspired to make some fundamental misunderstandings about how things actually worked.

As part of the Catholic Church, we were required to go to confession at intervals. We would go to a small, darkened room at the back of the church, and wait for the priest who was hearing confessions turn his attention to us. This was done individually, with the priest in a separate little room next to the one we would confess (to him) in. You did not see the priest face to face, you saw an outline of him through some rough surfaced glass, though you could hear him clearly enough (or so I thought). When it was your turn to confess, you did so; you told him the sins you had committed since the last time you confessed. He would then assign you a penance, and forgive you of your sins. Even as a child, all that was cut and dried, and very clear to me; I had been through it dozens of times.

One day, without any fanfare, a change occurred in the procedure. It completely flummoxed me. I had just entered the confessional, and was waiting my turn with the priest, when I noticed a white, wall-mounted telephone in front of me. It was to the left of the little window the priest would use to speak to people confessing. Though it was an extremely common item in 20th century America, I was completely floored to see it in a confessional. Why was there a phone there?

While I was waiting for the priest to speak to me, I tried to think of the reason that a telephone would be in here with me. After a while, I thought I had the answer. If the problem (or sin) was of the usual variety, the priest would handle it in the usual way, by speaking through the window directly to the one who was confessing. However, if your sin was particularly bad, God would intervene, by speaking to you directly, instead of through the priest. He would do this by phone, calling you in the confessional. While it was satisfying to have (so I thought) figured this out, it set me up for a far greater worry.

What would He be like to speak to? What happened if the phone rang, and I didn't answer? God could do anything, so He could speak to me without using a phone. But why did He use the phone? I thought as a courtesy to His creations; communicating with them through something familiar, instead of out of thin air. But if the phone rang, and He was on the other end, I was in BIG trouble.

Suffice it to say, every time I went to confession after that, I sweated blood waiting for that phone to ring. I literally prayed that it would not. For a while I thought my prayers had been answered, or at least I hadn't done anything so bad He needed to speak to me. Either way, I felt relieved, as the phone never rang. (It was years later I learned that the phone was for the hard of hearing, and it had a special amplifier to make the priest's voice easier to hear.) God works in mysterious ways.

Snapshot

Even as a child my mind worked differently than others' minds, child or adult. And, while my thinking was often logical, it was, at times, *wrong*. Again, there is that seemingly innocent expression, a little knowledge is a dangerous thing. Since then, I've learned better, though I still fall victim to it once in a while.

Once, during my early years in grade school, I saw a telegram a relative had received recently; he had brought it to a gathering at my grandparents' home. It was from someone they knew who lived in Canada. I was fascinated with it, because though the message was short and unremarkable, each sentence ended with the word "STOP". Fantastic!! I concluded that Canadians didn't use periods at the ends of their sentences. That was so different from how we did things in the U.S.!!

I couldn't wait to tell people about this, and I soon had told dozens of people, including many of the other students at my school. They were all fascinated with this, and I was more than happy to repeat the story to all who would listen. However, one day while I was telling this story to a group of students in one of my classes, I was struck by a thunderbolt from heaven.

A student in the back of the room piped up, and said very clearly, "I get letters from someone in Canada, and he uses periods; we're pen-pals". I stopped dead; instinctively knowing what he said was true. It then became clear to me; the telegram had "STOP" at the end of each sentence because that was how telegrams were written; it had nothing to do with being Canadian. Oh well, a little knowledge is a dangerous thing. I spent the next several months living that mistake down.

Snapshot

I knew at an early age that just because you were an adult, it didn't mean you knew how to reason properly, or that you could deal with problems properly. I was often shocked by how often adults would arrive at completely wrong, and even grossly stupid, "solutions" to problems that I could clearly see the correct answer to.

It took me some years after childhood before I could understand that part of the problem for most people, was their inability to accept circumstances (or problems) as they really were. So they would pretend to address a problem by imagining the problem to be much less than it really was, and then designing a solution for the miniaturized version of the real problem. Often, that solution was to let someone else deal with the problem.

One of the best examples of this type of aberrant thinking occurred when I was fourteen years old. I was working as a dishwasher at a local restaurant, and my Friday shift went to 2:00 A.M. This was in total violation of the labor laws of the time, for someone my age. However, I wanted the money and wasn't going to say anything to jeopardize my job.

So, I had an introduction early in my life to the kinds of people who were out late at night and early in the morning, and how they acted. It was a grand eye opener. Each shift the late night and early morning customers included a parade of drunks, drug abusers, and small-time criminals. But, the owner of the store wanted every last penny he could get, and wouldn't turn away anyone who might buy something. Eventually, I got used to it.

One night, just after closing at 2:00 A.M., one of the waitresses left to get to her car in the parking lot. She returned a few minutes later, with a peculiar expression on her face. Several of the employees, including me, were standing at the front counter when she came back in. She said simply, "my car won't start".

Several of the adult cooks went outside to see what was wrong, and I went with them. Even at my age, I had some knowledge of cars, and I thought the problem was something simple, like a weak or dead battery, a bad starter, a loose or corroded battery cable, or even that the car was out of gas. However, when we got to where her car was parked, we were completely shocked.

It looked like a *T. Rex* had stomped it. All four tires were flat, the windshield had been broken out, and the hood had been bent inwards, and then pried away from the hinges, so it stood almost straight up in front of the now absent windshield. The engine looked like it had been clubbed with a sledgehammer; the air cleaner was gone, and the carburetor had been beaten apart. All the major cables and hoses had been torn out of the engine, and thrown on the ground. The headlights and the taillights had been broken, the upholstery had been slashed, and there were gouge marks on the body panels from a screwdriver.

I stood in awe for a few moments of the damage that had been done to the car. I also almost immediately marveled at the mindset of someone who, after seeing such massive damage to their car, would get in it and try to start it as if nothing had happened. Then, after failing to start the car, coming back in to the restaurant and reporting the problem like it was something trivial. I thought that bordered on lunacy, or maybe idiocy. I couldn't understand how an adult could handle things so badly.

What was worse was the identity of the person who had done the damage. Not only did she know the person who had destroyed her car, it apparently was her ex-husband. At the time I was unfamiliar with the term "stalking", but I was introduced to it that evening. Someone, often known to you, followed you consistently, and at times acted against you, sometimes aggressively. Yes, this woman was being stalked by her ex-husband.

About a half-dozen of us stood around the car under the glare of the parking lot lights, trying to figure out if we could get the car's engine started, and get it to limp across the street to an all-night service station (back then, there were service stations that provided mechanics, and some would be on duty all night). That proved impossible, so we all pushed and heaved the car on four flat tires out of the parking lot, and into the service station. One of the guys stayed with the woman who owned the car, to make sure the mechanic knew what kinds of repairs were needed, and that she had a ride home.

I went home a bit later, thinking on that chilly night, that graduation into adulthood did not confer the ability to think properly, to act wisely, and to even have common sense. I considered the possibility that some people, no matter how old they became, would never be able to properly think for themselves. I hoped that would not happen to me.

<u>Snapshot</u>

I took religion seriously, even at a young age, and was not nearly as dismissive of it as others of my age. I would never think to mock any aspect of it, especially something that was very close to God. I truly feared Divine reprisal, and felt that God was constantly watching to see if we got out of step. Thus, an incident one summer shocked me to the very marrow of my bones.

The neighborhood children and I had made an excursion to the local creek; it was usually well-populated with tadpoles, frogs, fish, turtles, and crayfish (or crawdads). We caught a number of things, including a rather large crayfish, measuring about eight inches long. After returning home with our prizes, we wondered next what to do.

Someone suggested (flippantly, I thought) that we crucify the large crawdad. The suggestion was met with extreme approval by everyone except me. I was unnerved that they would mock the crucifixion, and that they seemed to have absolutely no idea of the seriousness of what they proposed. I argued vigorously against it, to no avail. The others quickly hammered together two sections of a medium-sized tree branch to make a cross. They extended the crawdad's claws like arms, and nailed them outstretched to the cross bar. They also nailed the crawdad's tail to the cross.

All the while during all this, they shouted "crucify him, crucify him!" I was practically sweating blood at this point, literally looking up at the sky, expecting a lightning bolt to come from heaven and annihilate us all. It rapidly got worse. The others made a procession, marching single file through the neighborhood, with the leader of the procession holding the cross the crawdad was nailed to. Everyone in line was chanting, "crucify him, crucify him".

I tried frantically to disrupt the procession and to stop it. I yelled that they were committing blasphemy, and that mocking the cross would be punished by God. They yelled back that they were not going to listen to me, because I thought that I knew everything, and that I did not speak for God. I gave up trying to convince them to stop their procession, and I ran home.

I literally hid under the bed, completely dressed (including my shoes) and shaking with fear, as I thought God was going to kill us all. Not being able to think rationally at the time, I should have known hiding under the bed would not have concealed me from Him, but I was scared. I stayed there for several hours, while I slowly recovered from my fright. It gradually became apparent to me that God was not going to do anything about this transgression, at least now right now.

I finally got up the nerve to crawl out from under the bed, looking around me before I moved the next foot. I finally got completely out, and stood up and looked out my bedroom window. The procession had ended, and the cross was lying in the back yard of the house directly behind ours. There was no trace of the crawdad. While it's possible he ascended to heaven on his death, I doubted that, thinking he had probably been pitched in the nearest garbage can.

I worked for the rest of the day on regaining my composure, and eventually regained my confidence to the point that I didn't have too many fears about what might happen to me while I slept. After that day, I never mentioned the crucifixion again, and in turn, I heard nothing about it.

<u>Snapshot</u>

It is true that religion had an outsized influence on my life in some ways, especially when compared to its influence on my peers, which was far less than on me. One reason religion influenced me so much was I tried to analyze it too much. It had not occurred to me during childhood that religion was taken on faith, not by analysis. God was not asking you to solve a riddle to believe in Him, He was asking you accept Him through belief. However, I was under the mistaken impression that one could literally reason one's way to God.

I visited my grandparents' home every Sunday, and on one Sunday I found a box of old slides which could be placed in a lighted slide viewer, which magnified the images several fold (though not as large as on a projection screen for home movies). They were pictures of the life of Jesus Christ, and showed him preaching and working miracles. I was amazed that these slides existed, and I was fascinated with what I thought was solid evidence of what He looked like.

Again, I was victim of the expression "a little knowledge is a dangerous thing". I didn't understand that the slides were photographs of recreations of Jesus' life, and that the photographs were taken recently. Should I have known better? I should have, considering in some of the pictures (where He was preaching in a field) there were telephone poles with telephone wires in the background.

Yes, I noticed them, but I came to two enormous erroneous conclusions. First, that they had cameras when Jesus was alive, and, second (because of the evidence in the background) they also had telephones back then too. It was quite logical, and quite wrong. But, I was not to know that for some time, or at least, to believe that.

For months after that, I was obsessed with finding some other evidence of telephones back in the time when Jesus walked the earth. I was constantly looking through books about the Old and New Testament, prayer books, books about religion in general, and hymnals, for pictures of telephones in antiquity. I often brought the books to mass and other church services; the nuns at school thought I was fervently praying.

And while I looked through many books, I never found a picture that looked even remotely like it had a phone in it. I broadened my search to look for pictures that showed just part of a phone, like the cord connecting the handset to the base, but I still found nothing. I just couldn't understand why I kept coming up empty. Still, my reasoning allowed for exceptions, like while telephones and telephone poles existed during the time of Christ, automobiles did not.

After some months I abandoned my search, though I still believed for a while that I just hadn't looked hard enough or long enough. Eventually, I forgot about it, though I later learned when the telephone was invented, and when the first telephone wires were strung. Oh well, so much for drawing conclusions based on limited information.

<u>Snapshot</u>

I've experienced a number of unsolvable mysteries in life, and they are more or less permanent fixtures in my memory, though I don't think about them that often. They are almost always simple things, yet they defy explanation of any rational sort. Usually, when I describe them to people, they simply dismiss them. I have never been offered any useful advice by anyone about how to explain the things I've experienced. At best, the "explanations" are whimsical.

So, by the time this event occurred, I already had a lengthy history of dealing with these kinds of things on my own. I was about ten years old when I was trekking through the local woods one day. Though the woods was right next door to the suburb we lived in, having extensive forested areas cheek-to-jowl with block housing was common, at least in the Midwest in the 1960s. The forested area I was walking through was one of the largest in the area, and despite my familiarity with it, I promptly got lost.

I knew I was lost because I saw terrain I had not seen before in this part of the woods, including a small stone peak, a wide stream, and even a burnt out portion of the forest. I was starting to get scared, wondering how long I would have to walk before I stumbled my way out by accident. And what would I do if I was still lost by the time night came? I pushed that thought out of my mind and forged on.

As I trudged steadily through the trees and the underbrush, my attention started wandering, so I had no clear idea how long I had walked before seeing something that stopped me dead. About ten yards in front of me was a small stand of trees, in a roughly circular pattern. Inside the border of trees was a clear space, mostly bare earth with some tufts of grass and weeds. On that clear space were five or six large heavy construction machines. One was a dump truck, another was a gravel spreader, and another was a road grader. I could not identify the others; while all of them had been there for a while, they did not appear to be antiques, as they looked similar to those I had seen in operation around our neighborhood recently.

I approached this land-locked version of the Bermuda Triangle cautiously, wondering if when I got close, the skeletal remains of the road crew would clamber out of the vehicles, the naked bones of their jaws yawning with hunger. However, nothing happened, even when I stood next to the dump truck. I watched and listened for a few minutes more, then climbed up onto the cab of the truck. I pulled the passenger door open with some difficulty, to find a moldy interior. I looked in the glove compartment, finding a rusted flashlight and some damp papers. I noted the keys were still in the ignition (I didn't try starting the truck).

Not finding the dump truck to be particularly interesting, I climbed out and down to the ground, to check out the other vehicles. Overall, they were much the same, festooned with large patches of rust and peeling yellow paint. Something about the vehicles bothered me, and I soon knew what it was. First, I couldn't see any traces of tracks, gouges, or tread marks to show the vehicles' path into the woods. I supposed it was possible that such evidence could have disappeared over time. Second, and much worse, they were in a cleared area surrounded by trees that were at least several decades old.

How could that be? These construction machines had not been here that long, maybe five or six years. How could they be surrounded by trees thirty or forty years old? Had the trees been cut down to make room for the heavy equipment, any trees that grew since then would still be saplings. I didn't understand that at all. Of course, the even larger problem was how did the vehicles get through the rest of the forest to get to this part of it. Many of the trees further away were huge, and probably several hundred years old.

The more I thought about it, the more confused I got. This simply wasn't possible, yet the construction equipment was here. And why would someone abandon the vehicles this way? It must have been a lot of time and effort to get them here. In some ways why they were here was worse than how they got here. Even at age ten, I knew some things worked in a certain way. When expensive equipment was retired, or even "junked", you just didn't dump it anywhere. It went to a scrapyard to be weighed and sold, after any usable parts were removed from it, either for use in vehicles like it that were still running, or were sold. Specific forms had to be filled out, and certain steps had to be taken. And, the disposition of the vehicles had to be verified; you just didn't take peoples' word for what had been done.

This just didn't make any sense. The vehicles just did not appear here one day by magic. They weren't airlifted in, either. I knew other people must have been through this part of the woods before me, as I had noticed candy bar wrappers and some rusty tin cans during my trek here. So why hadn't someone talked about this? If they had, it would have common knowledge in my neighborhood. I had a first-rate mystery here, and I had made zero progress in solving it.

I turned and left the clearing, vowing to myself to come back with a camera to take pictures of all this (I never did). I concentrated on getting out of the woods, and before I had gone more than several hundred yards, I found a narrow gravel road. I picked a direction, and followed that road; after about a mile, I saw a few houses in the distance, and the woods had thinned a bit. Another mile or so, and I saw a paved road intersect the gravel road; the paved road was marked with a street sign. I recognized the name of the street, and now knew where I was.

It took me about another hour and a half to walk home, just about in time for the sun to set. My parents didn't ask me where I'd been; they didn't really care. I didn't tell them about what I'd found in the woods, and I didn't tell anybody else, either. There didn't seem to be any point. I just filed the event in the mental "unknown" folder I had, and let it sit there, though every once in a while I pulled it out and looked at it.

<u>Snapshot</u>

This last entry differs from all those before it, because it is an account of a dream I once had. Everything else was an actual occurrence. Even so, the dream has many of the features of events I experienced in my waking moments. So, you can judge this event the same way as any of the others.

This dream occurred, in all places, in Russia. At least, that's what I thought I knew as I was dreaming. I was driving a semi-truck along a highway during the winter; snow was piled high along both sides of the road. It was afternoon and there was very little traffic. I saw no speed limit signs, but I felt I was not speeding. After a time I noticed a police car behind me, and it started flashing its lights.

I pulled over to the side of the road and the police car stopped behind me. I got out of the truck and the police officers were already there, standing on the shoulder of the road to meet me. I approached to within several feet, and one of them held up his hand, indicating no closer. I stood and waited. One of the spoke and I had no trouble understanding him, though I knew no Russian. (It was a dream, after all.)

He asked me what was in the truck. I answered, "bananas". His next question was perfectly reasonable. "If your truck is full of bananas, why does it say coconuts on the side?" I looked at the truck's trailer, and it did indeed have a large sign on it saying coconuts. I didn't have an answer for that. The policeman ordered me to unload the truck, so they could see what was in it.

I spent the next three or four hours unloading bunches and stalks of bananas from the truck; I made quite a pile on the road. I was getting exhausted when the policeman told me to stop; he was convinced that the only thing in the truck was bananas. I started to put the bananas back in the truck, but the policeman told me to leave them on the pavement. He told me to get back in my truck and follow them to the police station. I climbed back in the cab, started the truck, and got behind them.

We were on the road for about 30 minutes before arriving at the police station. It was not much to look at, a rather featureless square gray building. I parked, got out of the truck, and was escorted in through the front entrance. For some reason, the building seemed much bigger on the inside. We walked through an extensive series of hallways to get to a small room, which had a small table and several chairs. We sat down across from each other, and the questioning started.

My impression during the dream was the questioning lasted several hours, but I remembered only a few of the questions, which seemed pointless, like "do you have a venereal disease?" In any case, when the questioning was done, the police officers seemed satisfied with my answers. They told me I was free to go, but I had to leave my truck in the impounding lot next to the building. I didn't really care about that, and I walked out of the room.

I saw a back door and started walking towards it. The police officers followed me out into the hallway and asked me where I was going. I nodded towards the back door and kept walking. They asked me if I had understood I had to leave the truck here. I told them I didn't mind, because my spaceship was parked out back. I pushed the back door open and walked to my spaceship; while they watched I climbed in, and flew away.

Epilogue

The events I described all really happened (except for the dream). They have isolated me to a fair degree from the company of the human race, as telling people about the events usually convinces them I am crazy. It is indeed an unfortunate indictment of the human race that anyone who is different from the common herd is rejected (and hard). There is also no appeal.

I came to understand that in my childhood, and I have lived with it ever since. I see no chance of that changing. So be it. I live the life I have with no apologies, and I enjoy the richness of it without shame. So, enter my world, if you dare, and if you feel you must leave, it is on you to go back to the pale, shallow imitation of life that you had.

www.ingramcontent.com/pod-product-compliance
Lightning Source LLC
Chambersburg PA
CBHW051939150726
47999CB00006B/2281